TRADITIONS AND CELEBRATIONS

INDEPENDENCE DAY

by Emily Raij

PEBBLE
a capstone imprint

Published by Pebble, an imprint of Capstone
1710 Roe Crest Drive, North Mankato, Minnesota 56003
capstonepub.com

Library of Congress Cataloging-in-Publication Data is available on the Library of Congress website.
ISBN: 9798875284618 (hardcover)
ISBN: 9798875284564 (paperback)
ISBN: 9798875284571 (ebook PDF)

Summary: On Independence Day, Americans celebrate their freedom. They remember when the Declaration of Independence was adopted on July 4, 1776. It said that the thirteen colonies in North America were free of British rule. Today, Americans celebrate on the Fourth of July by having parades, lighting fireworks, and gathering at festivals. Readers will learn about the history of Independence Day and its many traditions.

Editorial Credits
Editor: Carrie Sheely; Designer: Heidi Thompson; Media Researcher: Rebekah Hubstenberger; Production Specialist: Tori Abraham

Image Credits
Capstone: Eric Gohl, 7; Dreamstime: Sara Winter, 25; Getty Images: Alex Wong, 1, 18, Ariel Skelley, 17, 20, Danielle Del Valle, 21, Eduardo Munoz Alvarez, 14, FOTOGRAFIA INC., 22, Hill Street Studios, 28, Hulton Archive, 12, Image Professionals GmbH, 27, iStock/Christine_Kohler, 9, iStock/Moussa81, 24, iStock/Roberto Galan, 15, Joe Raedle, 5, kali9, 23, Noam Galai, 19, PhotoSparks, 16, Vernon Lewis Gallery/Stocktrek Images, 11, ZU_09 6; Library of Congress: Prints & Photographs Division, 8, 13; Shutterstock: Billion Photos, cover

Design Elements
Shutterstock: Rafal Kulik

Printed and bound in China. 006459

TABLE OF CONTENTS

Words in **bold** are in the glossary.

What Is Independence Day?

People line the streets. They wave American flags. Marching bands play music. Parade floats go by. Later, families have picnics and barbecues.

At night, the sky glows with fireworks. *Pop*! It is the Fourth of July, also known as Independence Day. People celebrate America's **freedom** all day long.

NOBLE
Matthew Corcoran
HANCOCK ME
ANAH
M.C. 12875

The history of Independence Day goes back to the 1600s. British **settlers** arrived in North America. Many were looking for freedoms they did not have in Great Britain. Some wanted religious freedom. Others wanted to earn money by trading. The settlers formed 13 British **colonies**.

Pilgrims left Britain to seek religious freedom. They arrived in North America in 1620.

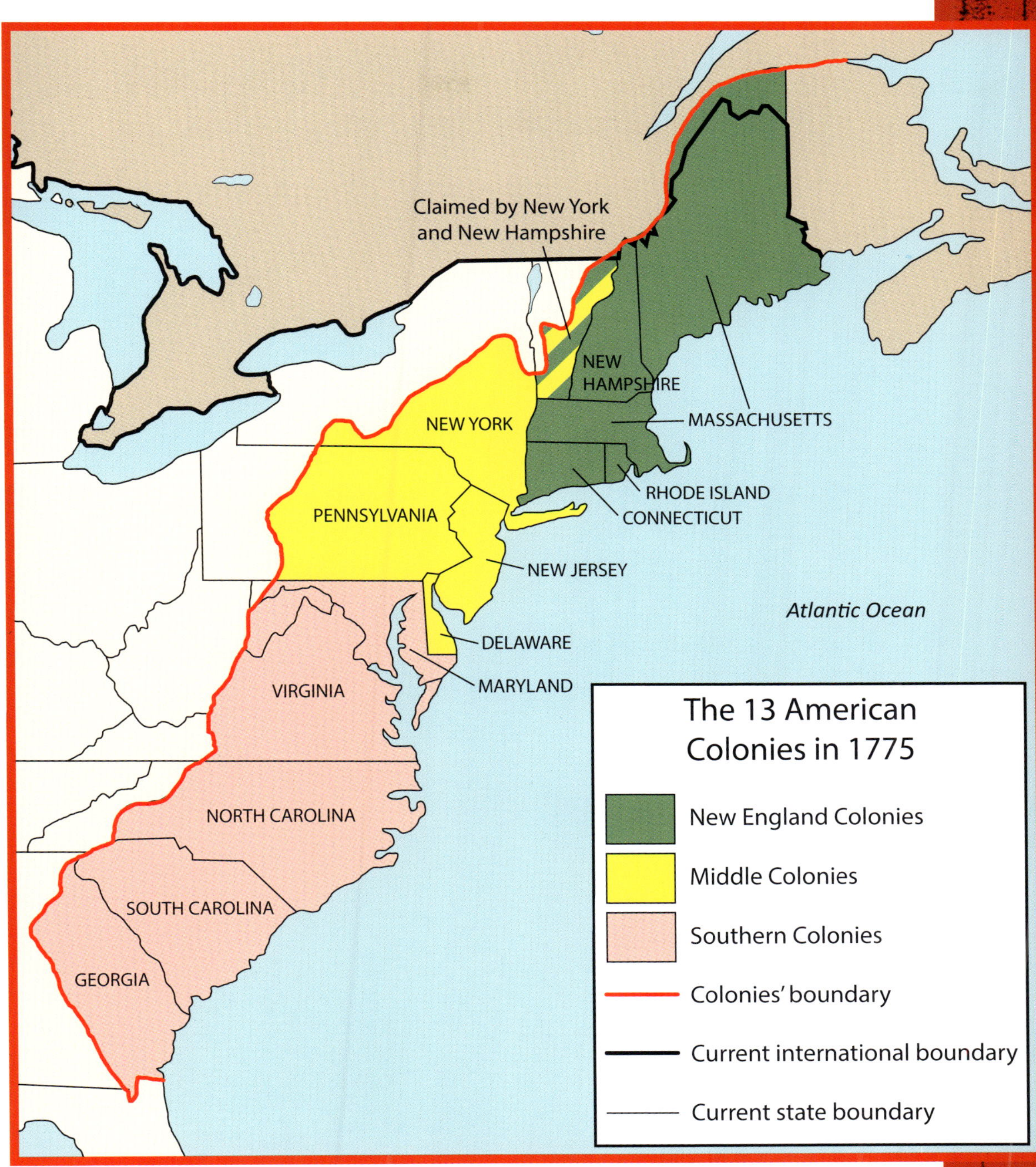
Claimed by New York and New Hampshire
NEW HAMPSHIRE
MASSACHUSETTS
NEW YORK
RHODE ISLAND
CONNECTICUT
PENNSYLVANIA
NEW JERSEY
Atlantic Ocean
DELAWARE
MARYLAND
VIRGINIA
NORTH CAROLINA
SOUTH CAROLINA
GEORGIA
The 13 American Colonies in 1775
New England Colonies
Middle Colonies
Southern Colonies
Colonies' boundary
Current international boundary
Current state boundary

The British King George III continued to rule the colonies. He did not let the colonists make decisions about their **government**. He also made the colonists pay taxes to Great Britain.

Over time, many colonists became angry. They began **protesting** British laws. After more conflicts, the Revolutionary War (1775–1783) started between the British and the American colonists.

King George III

Colonists protested against the Stamp Act in 1765. It taxed many printed materials such as newspapers and other items in the colonies.

In 1776, the colonists made a big decision. America would be a free nation. Colonial leader Thomas Jefferson wrote the draft of the Declaration of Independence. It explained why the colonies wanted to be free. John Adams and others made changes to the document.

Members of the Second Continental Congress approved it on July 4, 1776. That is considered America's birthday. The 13 colonies were now considered to be states.

Thomas Jefferson, John Adams, and other leaders present the Declaration of Independence draft to the Second Continental Congress.

Great Britain did not accept America's independence, and the war continued. Finally, the colonists won in 1783. George Washington became the first U.S. president.

Independence Day Celebrations

In 1797, John Adams became the second American president. He wrote a letter to his wife in 1776 about Independence Day. He thought it would be celebrated each year with parades. It still is!

A Fourth of July celebration in the mid-1800s

In 1876, a July Fourth celebration was held in Union Square, New York. It celebrated 100 years since the formation of the U.S.

The first Independence Day celebrations took place in Boston and Philadelphia in 1777. They were similar to today's celebrations. There were parades and fireworks. Bells rang. Leaders made speeches. In Pennsylvania, U.S. ships shot 13 cannons in honor of the 13 states.

New York City's Fourth of July fireworks show

Today, some places are known for their Fourth of July festivities. People travel to New York City for its fireworks show. The skies light up with bright colors.

Washington, D.C., has a big parade. Thousands of people line the streets. Military members and **veterans** march in the parade. **Patriotic** floats with red, white, and blue decorations travel by. Marching bands play songs such as "The Star-Spangled Banner." It is the national anthem, or song, of America.

The U.S. Army Old Guard Fife and Drum Corps march in the Fourth of July parade in Washington, D.C.

July Fourth is a **federal** holiday. U.S. government offices are closed. So are banks and post offices. Local businesses and government offices may close too.

Families and friends often celebrate together. Some gather at parks. Others get together in their backyards.

Boom! Many cities have their own fireworks shows. The colorful fireworks light up the sky. People watch a safe distance away in fields and parks. They bring picnic blankets and chairs. Sometimes patriotic music plays. The fireworks can even be set to music!

A fireworks show in Jersey City, New Jersey

Red, white, and blue are everywhere on the Fourth of July! Many people hang an American flag outside their home. Festive lights, wreaths, and balloons add color and fun to any party. People wear clothes showing the U.S. flag or with the flag's colors.

A Fourth of July concert in Nashville, Tennessee

The Fourth of July is a busy time to travel. Beaches are popular places to go for the holiday. So are concerts and parks. Some people go camping.

Independence Day Foods

Fourth of July celebrations include a lot of food! Barbecues and picnics almost always have hot dogs. People grill hamburgers and chicken too. Don't forget the buns, ketchup, mustard, and pickles! Corn on the cob, coleslaw, and potato salad are popular side dishes.

Summer means watermelon is in season! It pairs well with any main dish.

Red, white, and blue foods fit the patriotic day. Some people arrange food so it looks like a U.S. flag. This can be done with fruit. But other food works too! How about a U.S. flag-themed platter made with white cheese, red tomatoes, and blue tortilla chips?

Is it a hot day? Red, white, and blue popsicles or slushies can help everyone cool off.

Independence Day Projects

Do you want to bring a delicious dessert to your Fourth of July picnic? A patriotic parfait is fun and easy. You can make one to share in a big dish. Use smaller bowls to make individual treats.

Start with blueberries. Spread whipped cream on top. Then add strawberries or raspberries for the red layer. Repeat these steps until the dish is full.

Make an American flag decoration to hang on a door. You need a white paper plate, red and blue paint, a paintbrush, and white star stickers.

Paint the top left quarter of the plate blue. Rinse the paintbrush. Then paint red stripes across the rest of the plate. Leave white space between each red stripe. Let the paint dry.

Now it's time to finish your flag! Place the white star stickers on the blue area. Tape the flag to your front door. You are ready to celebrate the Fourth of July!

GLOSSARY

colony (KAH-luhn-ee)— an area that has been settled by people from another country; a colony is ruled by another country

federal (FED-ur-uhl)—the central government of the United States

freedom (FREE-duhm)—the right to live the way you want

government (GUHV-urn-muhnt)—the group of people who make laws, rules, and decisions for a country or state

patriotic (pay-tree-OT-ik)—showing love of and loyalty to one's country

protest (pro-TEST)—to object to something strongly and publicly

settler (SE-tuhl-uhr)—a person who makes a home in a new place

veteran (VE-tuh-ruhn)—person who served in the armed forces

READ MORE

Black, Sonia W. *If You Were a Kid at the Declaration of Independence*. New York: Scholastic, 2025.

Spanier, Kristine. *Independence Day*. Minneapolis: Jump! Inc., 2023.

Wyman, Kylie. *It's the Fourth of July!* Wauwatosa, WI: Orange Hat Publishing, 2024.

INTERNET SITES

Ben's Guide to the U.S. Government: From Colonial Rule to Independence
bensguide.gpo.gov/m-from-colonial-rule

Country Home: Interesting Fourth of July Facts for Kids
countryhomelearningcenter.com/interesting-fourth-of-july-facts-for-kids

National Geographic Kids: Independence Day
kids.nationalgeographic.com/history/article/independence-day

INDEX

ABOUT THE AUTHOR

Emily Raij has written more than 50 books for children and edited dozens of professional resources for K-12 teachers. She is a native of Chicago, where she earned her journalism degree from Northwestern University. She lives in Florida with her husband, daughter, son, and dog.